WHAT'S NEXT?

WHAT'S THE OPPOSITE?

A TURN-AND-SEE BOOK

by Cari Meister

PEBBLE
a capstone imprint

Opposites are everywhere!
A fire is hot. Ice cubes are cold.
Hot and cold are opposites.
Cotton candy is sweet.
Lemons are sour. Sweet
and sour are opposites.

Let's discover more opposites!
Read the text, look at the
picture, and guess the
opposite. Then turn the page
and see if you are right!

Raj and Amy are lifting weights in gym class. It is a lot of work! The weights are **heavy**!

What is the opposite of heavy?

turn and see

Light! Carolina lifts Mr. Cuddles into the air. He is light and fluffy.

It is a beautiful afternoon for a **slow** walk home from school. Jiah and Aiden take their time and enjoy the weather.

What is the opposite of slow?

turn and see

Fast! Max runs fast to launch the kite in the air. Whoosh!

Rishan picks out three chapter books from the library. Right now the books are **closed**.

What is the opposite of closed?

turn and see

Open! These kids couldn't wait to open their books!

The Harris kids are playing in the park. They jump **over** the rope.

What is the opposite of over?

turn and see

Under! Kaleb leads the relay team. He crawls under the foam noodles. Go, Kaleb, go!

Dara loves horses! She gets a giant stuffed horse for her birthday. She is **happy**.

What is the opposite of happy?

turn and see

Sad. Maisy cannot go with her older sister to camp. She is sad.

Yum! The Allen family is roasting marshmallows over a hot campfire.

What is the opposite of hot?

turn and see

Cold! The Yazzie cousins bundle up for a cold day of sledding. Ready, set, go!

Kezzie patiently waits her turn. The light is red, and red means stop.

What is the opposite of stop?

turn and see

Go! Kezzie hits the gas as soon as the light turns green. Zoom!

It's game day! **Before** the game, the team meets in a huddle.

What is the opposite of before?

turn and see

After! After the game, the team celebrates!

Sun and sand are all you need for a fun beach day! Dreyana and her mom are making a **small** sandcastle.

What is the
opposite of small?

turn and see

Big! Wow! Look at Trevon and Hailey's sandcastle!

Samir is thirsty after playing outside. He fills his cup to the top. The cup is full.

What is the opposite of full?

turn and see

Empty. Sean gulped down all of his milk. Now the glass is empty.

Woof! Woof! Buster is getting a bath. He is very **wet**!

What is the opposite of wet?

turn and see

Dry! Tita's dog, Mr. Pickles, ran outside in the rain. Tita used a warm towel to dry him off.

It's street art **day**! The neighborhood kids from Sunny Drive create a chalk picture.

What is the opposite of day?

turn and see

Night! John and Sidney get ready to camp for the night. Sleep tight!

On a hot summer day, Emi splashes in her **shallow** pool.

What is the opposite of shallow?

turn and see

Deep! Noah and his friends dive into the deep end of the pool.

Wah! Wah! Baby Avery is hungry.
She is loud!

What is the
opposite of loud?

turn and see

Quiet. Shhh. Baby Quentin is sleeping.

OPPOSITES REVIEW

- heavy/light
- slow/fast
- closed/open
- over/under
- happy/sad
- hot/cold
- stop/go
- before/after
- small/big
- full/empty
- wet/dry
- day/night
- deep/shallow
- loud/quiet

Pebble Sprout is published by Pebble, an imprint of Capstone.
1710 Roe Crest Drive
North Mankato, Minnesota 56003
www.capstonepub.com

Library of Congress Cataloging-in-Publication Data
Names: Meister, Cari, author.
Title: What's the opposite? : a turn-and-see book / by Cari Meister.
Other titles: What is the opposite?
Description: North Mankato, Minnesota : Pebble, an imprint of Capstone, [2021] | Series: Pebble Sprout: What's next? | Audience: Ages 6-8. | Audience: Grades 2-3 | Summary: "Wah! Wah! A crying baby is loud. But what about a sleeping baby? You guessed it! A sleeping baby is quiet. With a flip of the page you will discover that opposites are everywhere"— Provided by publisher.
Identifiers: LCCN 2020037978 (print) | LCCN 2020037979 (ebook) | ISBN 9781977131560 (hardcover) | ISBN 9781977155320 (ebook pdf) | ISBN 9781977156945 (kindle edition)
Subjects: LCSH: English language—Synonyms and antonyms—Juvenile literature. | Polarity—Juvenile literature.
Classification: LCC PE1591 .M458 2021 (print) | LCC PE1591 (ebook) | DDC 428.1—dc23
LC record available at https://lccn.loc.gov/2020037978
LC ebook record available at https://lccn.loc.gov/2020037979

Image Credits
Getty Images: FatCamera, 3; Imgorthand, 28, kali9, 7; Obradovic, 24; PeopleImages, 19; THEPALMER, 23; Shutterstock: Alexander_Safonov, 4; ALIAKSANDRKAZLOUSKY, 12; Asia Images Group, 11; BNMK 0819, 22; Brocreative, 5; Jaren Jai Wicklund, 14; leungchopan, 29; mantinov, 27; oliveromg, 13; Peyker, 15, 16; Pixel-Shot, 30; Pond Saksit, 9; Rawpixel.com, 17, 18; RonTech3000, 26; Sergey Novikov, 6, 10, 20, 25; Shyamalamuralinath, 21; tdee photo cm, cover; wavebreakmedia, 8

Editorial Credits
Editor: Christianne Jones; Designer: Tracy McCabe; Media Researcher: Morgan Walters; Production Specialist: Kathy McColley

Printed and Printed in the United States 5695